Cartooning for Kids!
Mashup Mania

By Dave Garbot

Publisher: Rebecca J. Razo

Creative Director: Shelley Baugh

Production Director: Yuhong Guo

Senior Editor: Stephanie Meissner

Managing Editor: Karen Julian

Developmental Editor: Janessa Osle

Editorial Assistant: Julie Chapa

Production Designer: Debbie Aiken

Illustrated and written by Dave Garbot

www.walterfoster.com

6 Orchard Road, Suite 100

Lake Forest, CA 92630

Printed in China

February 2015

1 3 5 7 9 10 8 6 4 2

19264

Table of Contents

What You Will Need

crayons

eraser

colored pencils

markers

pencil

Drawing paper

Getting Started

A hippo with wings? A fish that's a boy? A monster mailman? Have you ever heard of such things? In this book we're going to take some ordinary creatures and combine them with some not-so-ordinary activities. It may sound crazy, but we'll have fun learning to draw them, and maybe you'll come up with some ideas of your own! Remember, anything goes—it's a total mashup!

Funky Features

Here are a few things you can use when drawing your characters. Maybe you'll want a different nose, beak, or tail! You can come back to these pages anytime you need some ideas.

Accessories

This beastly beauty queen loves to accessorize, and many of the characters we'll be drawing do too. Come back to these pages if your character needs a different hat, a fluffy pair of slippers, or even a slice of pizza to go with their ensemble!

Unlikely Pairs

In this section we'll learn to draw characters such as a cat, skunk, and hippo. They may seem normal at first, but they're doing things that we would never imagine them doing. Let's mash them together! Have you ever seen an elephant wear a tutu or a rhino bake a cake? It's crazy!

Fish Boy

How would Fish Boy look with a different tail? Start with an upside-down cone shape tilted a little to the left.

Betty Ballerina

How would Betty look with a different color tutu? Move the groundline lower so that it doesn't touch Betty's foot, and it will look like she's jumping!

Lion Librarian

How would this lion look with a hat?
Go back to page 10 if you need an idea.

19

Skunky School Teacher

Can you make this skunk hold something else?
How about an apple, a banana, or a fish?

Robot Kitty

How would this kitty look with his arms drawn up in the air instead of down? Give it a try! If you draw your shapes tilted a little to the left or right, kitty will look like he's moving!

Meow. Meow. Meow.

Meow. Meow. Meow.

23

Guinea Pig Princess

This princess is so cute! How would she look
with some groovy sunglasses?

Snaky Prince Charming

Have you ever seen a snake with spots or stripes? Give it a try! Start out with a simple rectangle, but don't make your lines too straight—snakes are kind of wobbly!

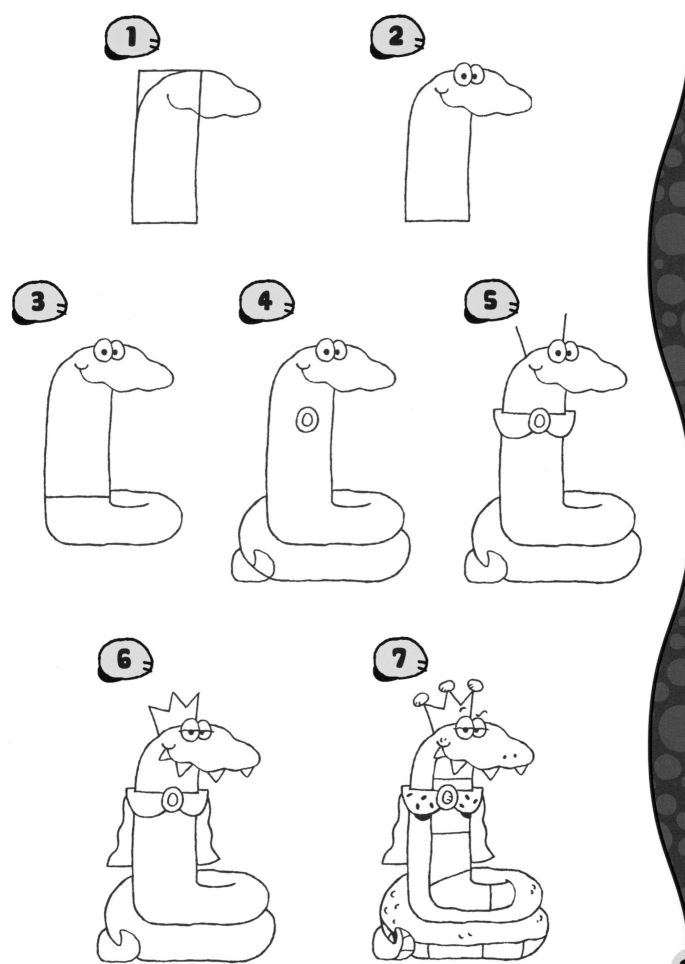

Flying Hippo

Can you draw this hippo without his goggles?

Roller Derby Cow

Can you give this crazy skater a different uniform and maybe a bigger helmet?

Rhino Baker

Can you draw something different on this baker's plate?
How about a pie or a big cookie! Also try adding more mice—
they're hungry!

Section Two

Even Less Likely Pairs

In this section we'll mash up even more ridiculous characters! A zombie playing a guitar? A snowboarding raccoon? Space chickens? This group is out of this world!

Alien Professor

Five eyeballs, but only two ears? Can you give the professor more ears? In step 1, draw the middle eye first, and then connect two eyes on each side of it.

Dr. Dracula

Can you give the professor more ears?
What else can you change?

Beastly Beauty Queen

How would Miss Beastie look with a small cowboy hat instead?
Try moving the middle line in step 1 higher or lower to see how
that affects your drawing.

1

2

3

4

5

6

MISS BEASTIE

Zombie Rock Star

How about adding some shades to this groovy ghoul? Drawing his hat off his head and his feet off the ground gives your zombie rock star crazy energy!

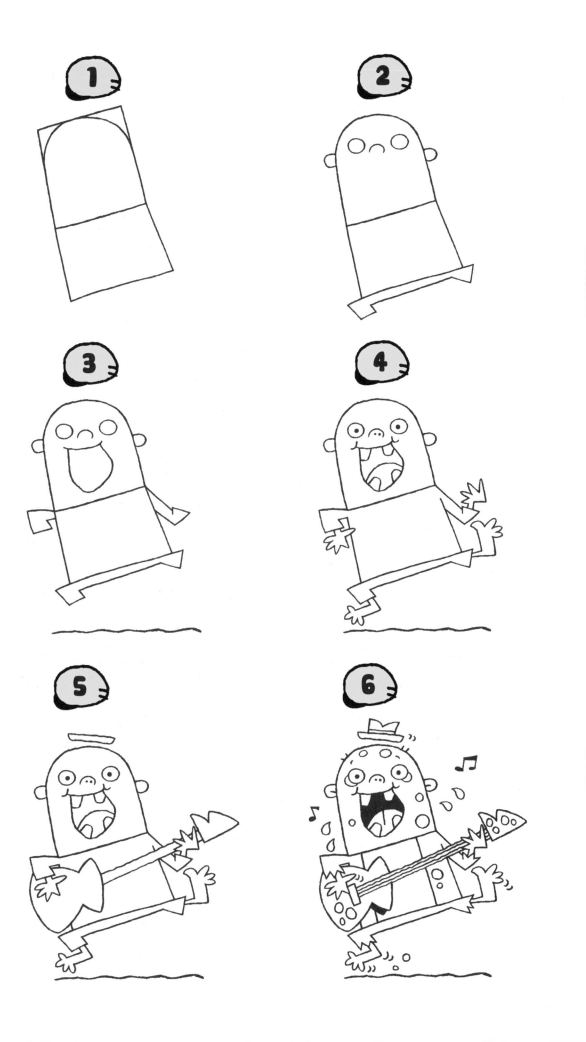

Ladybug Superhero

Should our hero have more spots? Start out with a big circle, but don't worry if it's wobbly—even superhero bugs are wobbly sometimes.

Dinosaur Cowgirl

This cowgal is pretty cute. Can you make her a different color? Giving your dino long eyelashes will make her look extra sweet!

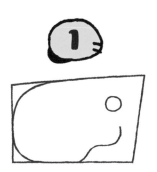

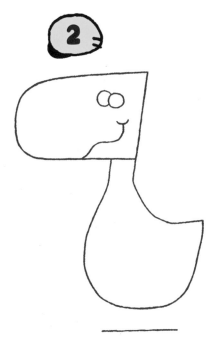

Farmer Panda

Can you add a few more chicks for this farmer to watch over? Keep your eraser handy—you'll need it to help this farmer take shape.

Racer Rabbit

After you draw one car and rabbit, try drawing more to make it a real race! Drawing the wheels on an angle and above the groundline will make your racer look like he's really moving!

Monster Mailman

This mailman is frantic! How would he look
with another eye and more teeth?

Skydiving Squirrel

Do you think this crazy squirrel needs a bigger or smaller parachute? Can you think of anything else he might need?

Sharky Lifeguard

Maybe this shark could use a hat. Go back to page 10 for an idea if you need one. Drawing the shape in step 1 taller, shorter, or even wider will completely change the look of your character.

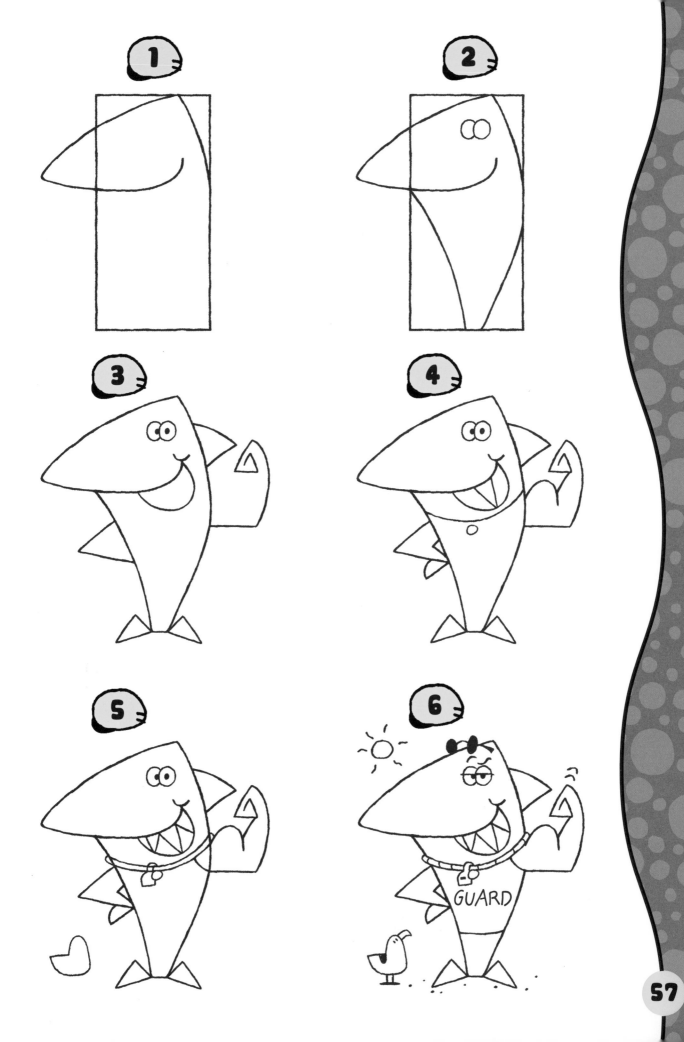

Warthog Waitress

This waitress is ready to take your order.
What can you change to make her look different?
New shoes, glasses, or maybe a hat?

Raccoon Snowboarder

Can you add a special design to this raccoon's board? Does he need mittens? In step 7, if you draw the groundline and the shadow lower than the board, it will make your raccoon look like he's airborne!

Astronaut Chickens

Can you add a few more floating chicks to this crazy group? Next time try drawing the big chicken upside down. Anything can happen in space!

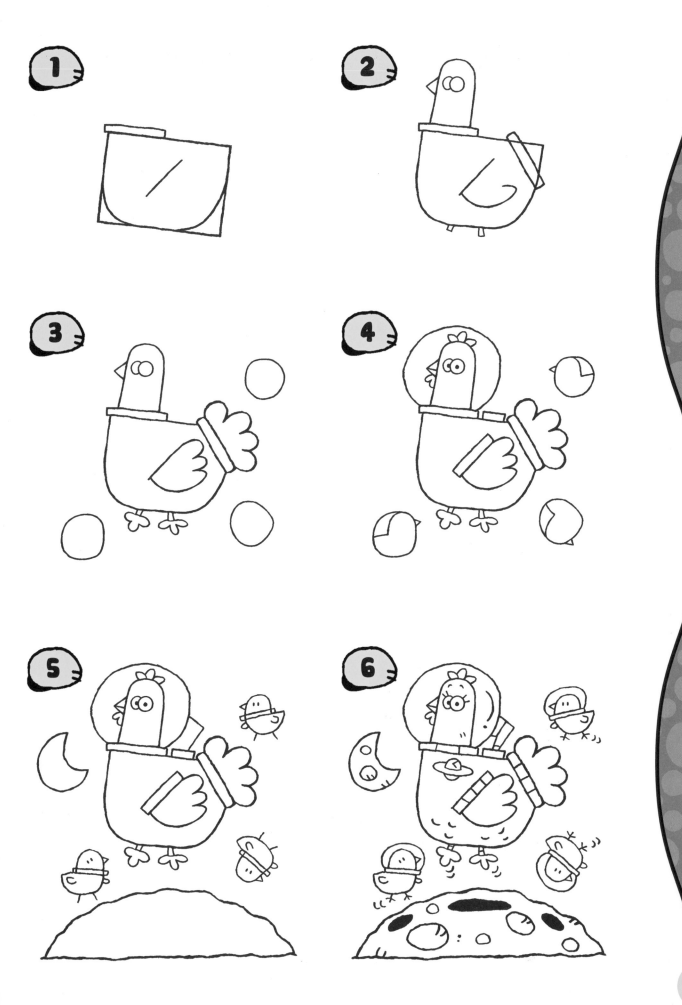

About the Author

Dave Garbot is a professional illustrator and has been drawing for as long as he can remember. He is frequently called upon to create characters for children's books and other publications. Dave always has a sketchbook with him, and he gets many of his ideas from the things he observes every day, as well as from lots of colorful childhood memories. Although he admits that creating characters brings him personal enjoyment, making his audience smile, feel good, and maybe even giggle is what really makes his day.

Dave is from Portland, Oregon, and you can see more of his work at www.garbot.com.